MAGNIFYING YOUR DAYS

MAGNIFYING YOUR DAYS

INSPIRATIONAL DEVOTIONALS FOR GRIEVING

Bonnie Rinehart

WINEPRESS WP PUBLISHING

Packaged by WinePress Publishing, PO Box 428, Enumclaw, WA 98022. The views expressed or implied in this work do not necessarily reflect those of WinePress Publishing. The author is ultimately responsible for the design, content, and editorial accuracy of this work.

Unless otherwise noted, all Scriptures are taken from the Holy Bible, New Living Translation, Copyright © 1996 by Tyndale Charitable Trust. Used by permission.

Scripture references marked KJV are taken from the King James Version of the Bible.

Scripture references marked NASB are taken from the New American Standard Bible, © 1960, 1963, 1968, 1971, 1972, 1973, 1975, 1977 by The Lockman Foundation. Used by permission.

ISBN 1-57921-450-9
Library of Congress Catalog Card Number: 2002100713

In loving memory of my mom,
Ruth Rinehart.
Her many prayers and strong faith continue to
impact my life.

I would also like to express my gratitude to Luella
Burroughs, who taught high school English to my
mom and me, for assisting with editing
"Magnifying Your Days."

—Bonnie Rinehart

Mom overjoyed at her first ever surprise birthday party at age 72. "Only God can make a rose."

Contents

Contents

Bonnie poses with her German Shepherd, Mel, in the backyard.

The eyes of the Lord search the whole earth in order to strengthen those whose hearts are fully committed to Him. (2 Chronicles 16:9)

But those who wait on the Lord will find new strength. They will fly high on wings like eagles. They will run and not grow weary. They will walk and not faint. (Isaiah 40:31)

A Time for Everything

Everything has a season.
Everything happens for a reason.
My life lived for God is never in vain.
Most of His molding is done through my pain.

There's a time to die and a time to shed tears.
He never leaves my side through all my years.
There's a time to lose and a time to turn away.
I dwell on what's left, not on what's lost on the way.

At times life brings changes that just don't seem right.
God has a better plan in store just out of my sight.
I walk by faith and believe my Father will give
only the best of everything as for Him I live.

Sometimes I have to wait as God leads.
Other times it's painful as my garden He weeds.
At times the flowers bloom oh so bright.
There's so much joy in knowing I'm doing what's right.

"I'm sure God has really big dreams for me," I pondered.
He gave me back all those years I had squandered.
It's time for me to dream big dreams too.
I'll praise God whatever comes 'til my last days are through.

Years ago I learned the value of focusing on what I have, not on what I've lost along life's way. If I live my life regretting what I've done in the past or worrying about what will happen in the future, I miss enjoying my life as it is right now. Daily I trust God as He leads me. When I have felt like the struggle is just too hard, I have learned to be still until the anxiety passes; and it always has. There are times when the very best decision I can make is to do absolutely nothing myself and rest in my assurance that God is in control of everyone and everything in my life. Experience has taught me that just around the corner is my blessing if I just hang on long enough to attain it. Not only is there joy in knowing I am doing God's will, but also there is joy in knowing that I am not hurting anyone else or myself in the process. It is in the hardest darkest times of my life that I have learned to lean and depend on God to help me get through my struggles. It is there that I have sought God, experienced His strength and love, and grown closer to Him. God is delighted when I am closer to Him today than I was yesterday.

Dear God, may your Holy Spirit draw me closer to You today than I was yesterday, as Your eyes search the whole earth to strengthen us whose hearts are fully committed to You. May I rest in the moment and trust because I know You have everything under control.

And we know that God causes everything to work together for the good of those who love God and are called according to His purpose for them. (Romans 8:28)

And let us run with endurance the race that God has set before us. We do this by keeping our eyes on Jesus, on Whom our faith depends from start to finish. (Hebrews 12:1–2)

Set your sights on the realities of heaven, where Christ sits at God's right hand in the place of honor and power. Let heaven fill your thoughts. Do not think only about things down here on earth. (Colossians 3:1–2)

Focus on Jesus

I knew my life would never be the same after Mom called that day.
She said she couldn't live with my dad. She just had to get away.
"There's no one to tell me what to do or even to yell at me!
I'm free at last! Such peace I've found! I'm free! I'm free!"

Funny how I could wake up one day and life could change overnight.
Life gets so hard. I can't find my way. Absolutely nothing seems right.
I can't find my peace, and this restlessness just will not go away.
Then I remember to surrender to God, and with thanks, I pray.

If you look too far ahead, life can overwhelm you with worry and fear.
God promises to give strength for the day, not the entire year!
Never forget to keep a list of blessings you are thankful for.
Read them often; praise God for them, always be looking for more!

I thank God for both the good and the bad that come into my life.
He's in control of each one of them, even my heartaches and strife.
He's tearing apart my heart and stretching it 'til I've grown.
He works all things for my good and calls me to be His own.

When life on earth gets tough to take,
When your heart is about to break,
My solution is free and really easy to find.
Open your Bible, and let heaven fill your mind!

Focus on Jesus and He'll do the rest.
This too shall pass, this trial, that test.
Only as pilgrims do we roam.
Heaven is our eternal home!

My real home is in heaven with loved ones so dear.
With God in control, I have nothing to fear.
"I'll have a brand new body made by God Himself for me.
I'll be free at last! Such peace I'll find! I'll be free! I'll be free!"

One of Mom's favorite sayings was, "I can live around a lot. I'm not going to let anything upset me." Many years ago Mom learned the key to being content. She focused on the solutions of life and not on the problems. Mom chose Jesus Christ as the focus of her entire life.

Jesus Christ is always greater than any problem I face today. The more I focus on Jesus Christ, the smaller my problem becomes and the bigger Christ becomes. When Jesus is at the center of my day and life, His love and peace permeate everything I do and everyone I touch. How comforting to know that God will cause everything in my life to work for good. Jesus loved me enough to die for me; I'll have a home in heaven with Him. This life will pass, along with all of its problems and heartaches, but in heaven I will live forever with my Creator and Redeemer, the almighty Lord Jesus Christ!

Ruth with her granddaughter, Jesse, enjoying the first spring tulips in Bonnie's front yard.

You will keep in perfect peace all who trust in You, whose thoughts are fixed on You! Trust in the Lord always, for the Lord God is the eternal rock. (Isaiah 26:3–4)

Those who become Christians become new persons. They are not the same anymore, for the old life is gone. A new life has begun. (2 Corinthians 5:17)

Therefore, since we are surrounded by such a huge crowd of witnesses to the life of faith, let us strip off every weight that slows us down, especially the sin that so easily hinders our progress. (Hebrews 12:1)

Transformation

Mom, when you first came to live with me,
Eyes full of pain and fear did I see.
As I placed fresh cut flowers all around your place,
Transformation slowly appeared upon your face.

I dug up half my front yard and placed flowers there too,
So you could have a beautiful living room view.
I set a table and chair out front for you to savor
All the tulips, daffodils, and other beauty from my labor.

Mom, how you enjoyed your backyard view!
There were trellises, arbors, and waterfalls too.
A fountain is surrounded by a hill of trees.
The many colored flowers dance in the breeze.

I can still hear you laugh as my dogs, wild and tense,
Chased those squirrels as they teased from the fence.
You told me you were sorry the day my dogs died.
I'd give anything, Mom, to have you back by my side.

How you loved to get up early in the morning to see
Which roses opened so you could show them to me!
You told me you cherished your time of peace and prayer.
You told God your troubles and left your burdens there.

The most beautiful sight I recall seeing there
Were monarch butterflies flying everywhere.
A great deal of love and respect to Mom I give.
She taught me to cherish life as I live.

I rise early to see which roses are new.
I cherish the memories of time spent with you.
"Mom, when I miss talking to you
I talk to God Who brings me through."

My mom left my father and moved in with me after forty-eight years of marriage. Mom's eyes were filled with fear and looked like those of an animal that had been caged up far too long. I set out at once to start nurturing Mom. I gave everything I had to make her feel cared for and loved. Over a period of time, Mom's eyes became filled with joy, peace and love. Everywhere Mom looked were beautiful flowers that God had created. Mom would take me to the back yard and show me each day which roses had opened. Mom always said, "Only God can make a rose."

Mom shared with me how she would sit in the arbor and talk with God. Now I talk to God and Mom in our flower garden as I recall all the wonderful moments we shared in my back yard praising God for His beautiful handiwork.

Mom's favorite variegated red and white rose opened yesterday. My eyes welled up with tears because Mom wasn't physically here to share that special moment with me. I looked up to the heavens and told Mom, "Look, your favorite rose is blooming." I believe Mom is with me in spirit everywhere I go. Then I smiled as I recalled asking God to give Mom a field of red roses with white baby's breath on Valentines Day. I asked God to write in the card for me, "Mom, I love you and I miss you. I can't wait until I can see your beautiful smiling face again." Imagine the magnificent aroma Mom experiences every day as she enjoys those roses. When I get to heaven, I can already hear Mom say, "Thanks a million!"

Ruth's siblings and parents.
Back row: Ruth, Emma, Mike, Marty, Eddie, Mary, and Anna.
Front row: Clara, Susie, parents Katie and William Hofer, Viola, and Betty.
"The Lord's loved ones are precious to Him; it grieves Him when they die" (Psalm 116:15).

Comfort—to strengthen in body and spirit. To console.

All praise to the God and Father of our Lord Jesus Christ. He is the source of every mercy and the God Who comforts us. He comforts us in all our troubles so that we can comfort others. (2 Corinthians 1:3–4)

And God will wipe away all their tears. (Revelation 7:17)

Even when I walk through the dark valley of death, I will not be afraid, for You are close beside me. (Psalm 23:4)

Not Today, Maybe Tomorrow

"Can we go home now?" were the words my mom said
Each and every day from her hospital bed.
"Not today, Mom, maybe tomorrow,"
Was the reply I gave her with utmost sorrow.

It wasn't the answer she wanted to hear.
"It's all right Mom. I'll stay ever so near.
It doesn't really matter if we're here or there.
Just so we're together with our love to share."

"Each other, that's all we have left." Mom said to me.
"We've been through a lot together, haven't we?"
Mom fondly smiled and placed her arm around me.
I promised to take good care of her and keep her pain-free.

I stayed by her side both day and night.
I didn't dare let her out of my sight.
My mom in pain I could not bear.
I was afraid she'd fall if I weren't there.

It broke my heart to leave Mom's side,
But I had to go when my father died.
I left Mom with my dear friend.
God provided to the very end.

As I returned to Mom's room that night,
I asked Mom if it would be all right
if I crawled in bed next to her and slept.
She replied, "I'd just love that," and I quietly wept.

I told her how much I loved her and held her all night long.
"You were a really good mom," I said as I sang her favorite song.
"God may take you to heaven soon. Is there anything left to do?"
Mom peacefully said she'd worked all of that through.

Mom, with a look of awe-filled peace,
Went home to heaven where her pain did cease.
When grief overwhelms me with all of its sorrow,
"Can I go home now?" "Not today, my child, maybe tomorrow."

Mom was in the hospital a total of fourteen days. She wanted to go home from day one. Each day I would tell her, "Not today, but we'll see how tomorrow goes." Mom was diagnosed with having had a major heart attack, strokes and congestive heart failure, while my father was in another hospital dying from lung cancer and congestive heart failure fifty miles away. I left Mom's side twice to attend Dad's funeral and prayer service. The night of Dad's funeral, Mom decided to sleep in her bed instead of her usual cardiac chair. *Why tonight of all nights?* I was so weary.

I asked Mom if it would be all right if I slept next to her. Mom gladly said yes, and I held her all night long as I quietly wept. This was one of those nights I would rather have been at home in heaven where I wouldn't have to feel this intense pain. I didn't know how much longer I would have her, so I decided to make every minute count. I am thankful I had that entire week to tell Mom everything in my heart regarding how much I loved and appreciated her. Cherish your loved ones every day. Don't be afraid to tell them that you love them and how much they mean to you. You don't know how long you will have to express your love for them.

Honor your father and mother. (Exodus 20:12)

O Lord, you have examined my heart and know everything about me. You know when I sit down or stand up. You know my every thought when far away. You chart the path ahead of me and tell me where to stop and rest. Every moment You know where I am. You know what I am going to say even before I say it, Lord. (Psalm 139:1–4)

Do They Know?

Do they know how she likes to move from her chair to her bed?
Do they know which pillow she likes under her head?
Do they know how to fluff that pillow just right?
Does their mere presence calm her in the middle of the night?

Do they know how many covers she likes around her waist?
Do they know she likes hot tea and just how to make it taste?
Do they know she likes that one certain lip balm?
Do they know her favorite passage is the 139th Psalm?

Do they know she likes CNN and the 700 Club?
Do they know she likes her hair brushed and a firm foot rub?
Do they know how much I love her and don't want her left alone?
Do they know how my heart breaks every time I hear her groan?

Do they know she loves her Bible and wants it within reach?
Do they know she didn't cry until she lost her speech?
Do they know I was helpless and full of despair?
Do they know I'd have given anything to take her place there?

Do they know that certain angle she likes to lie back in her chair?
Do they know she needs elbow pads, so she won't get sore there?
Do they monitor her pain and know how to make it quit?
Do they know when to give her medicine and when to hold it?

You see, I'm not just the nurse this time.
This isn't just another patient of mine.
When they tell me to sleep or I'll burn out,
It's my mom, not me, I worry about.

Do they know how strong her faith is and that she's ready to die?
Do they know how much she wants to look Jesus in the eye?
Do they know she always said there are worse things than death?
Do they know I held her hand when she took her last breath?

When Mom lost her ability to speak after the first week of her hospitalization, Brenda and I were both there to comfort her. We reassured Mom that we knew what her needs were and that we would do our very best to meet them. It broke our hearts to see all that fear and helplessness in Mom's eyes that day. We also felt a tremendous amount of helplessness as each day Mom's condition became worse. I reassured Mom that God knew her thoughts and that she was never alone.

How reassuring to know that God knows everything about me and thinks about me all the time. In the morning when I awaken, He is still thinking about me. Brenda and I were very thankful to be able to support Mom on that particularly difficult day. I learned to leave Mom in God's hands and trusted Him to keep her safe in my absence. Whenever I would begin to worry about Mom when I was at home, I would pray and release her to God to comfort and protect her.

No eye has seen, no ear has heard, and no mind has imagined what God has prepared for those who love Him. (1 Corinthians 2:9)

You will show me the way of life, granting me the joy of Your presence and the pleasure of living with You forever. (Psalm 16:11)

A Gift from God

What a wonderful gift God gave me that night.
Mom's eyes opened. Oh, what a sight!
Her eyes opened wide as her jaw dropped in awe.
I often wonder and ponder what she saw.

An amazing thing happened on Mom's last night.
For over thirty seconds she stared at a sight.
"Mom's waking up," I cried,
As her faithful Bridegroom arrived for His bride.

When I thought Mom had taken her last gasp of air,
I closed her eyes with gentle, loving care.
She opened her eyes again and surprised me.
She wasn't done gazing at what she wanted to see.

Mom's biggest hope was about to take place.
She always talked about seeing Jesus' face.
I cheered Mom on to see Jesus as her pain went away.
God answered our prayers and took Mom home that day.

It was Mom's thirteenth day in the hospital. She had been unresponsive the four days prior. Mom's breathing was slowing down as death was near. Family was notified of Mom's declining status. Right before Mom died, for thirty seconds, she opened her eyes as wide as they could possibly go. At the same time, her jaw dropped so far down that her face appeared distorted because it was such a peaceful awe. Each movement she made was extremely slow and methodical, like that of a robot. I have a hard time even finding words to explain the look on Mom's face. It was like none I have ever seen before. I believe what Mom saw was Jesus Himself coming to take her to heaven. I believe He was so magnificent that Mom's earthly body could hardly contain His extraordinary presence.

The nurses taught me that it is helpful to give permission to the dying patient to leave this world and move on to the next. Right after Mom took her last gasp of air, I told her, "You go to heaven, Mom. You go ahead and go." Who would have ever dreamed I would be cheering Mom on to heaven. Thank God for His perfect plan of salvation for each one of our lives and that special gift of my knowing Mom did not leave this world alone. After Mom died, I found a poem in her Bible called "Safely Home." One of the stanzas in this poem seems to best describe what I believe was happening in that thirty second span of time. "All the pain and grief is over. Every restless tossing passed; I am now at peace forever safely home in heaven at last. And He came Himself to meet me in that way so hard to tread; And with Jesus' arm to lean on, could I have one doubt or dread?"

And the main street was pure gold, as clear as glass. (Revelation 21:21)

Don't be troubled. You trust God, now trust in Me. There are many rooms in my Father's home, and I am going to prepare a place for you. If this were not so, I would tell you plainly. When everything is ready, I will come and get you, so that you will always be with Me where I am. (John 14:1–3)

Streets of Gold

When flooded with deepest grief,
I pray for God to comfort me.
I experience such sweet relief
As He sets me free.

My tears fall like rain
As I begin to pray.
God shares my pain,
As He wipes my tears away.

God is my faithful Healer of Light.
He takes every burden and care.
I ask Him to hold me in the middle of the night.
Each and every time, He meets me there.

He brings comfort and calming peace to me
As I surrender to His loving ways,
I thank God for setting me free.
He inhabits my praise for the rest of my days.

"Don't cry for me when I die.
Walking on streets of gold is where I'll be!"
I recall that deep faith in her eye.
It comforts and strengthens me.

God was merciful, sovereign and just
When He took Mom to heaven that night.
Mom is safe in Your arms—that I trust.
She's not dead. She's alive in Your healing light!

Jesus holds me in His nail-pierced hand.
Never to leave is His promise to me.
From the truth in His Word I take my stand.
"Walking those streets of gold, someday I'll be!"

One day, I was sitting upstairs with Mom in her living room and admiring the two pictures we had picked out together. One picture was a house with a door as the focal point, which had John 14:1–3 as the caption. Another picture was of a woman picking flowers and laying them in a basket. That caption was from Mom's favorite song, "In the Garden." "God walks with me and talks with me and tells me I am His own. And the joys we share as we tarry there, none other has ever known." I told Mom what neat keepsakes those pictures would be someday. Mom told me not to cry for her when she died because she was ready to see Jesus and go to heaven. She radiated with joy when she confidently added, "I'll be walking on streets of gold!" Mom's life had been filled with so much pain. She longed for the good life to come where there would be no more tears of disappointment in her life. Praise God, who agonized on the cross to the point of death and rose again three days later, so that someday I will be able to be with Mom again. I imagine Mom walking in the fullness of God's love, peace and joy on those streets of gold. This very second as I type what peace and joy that thought brings to my heart!

Ruth embracing her granddaughter, Mel.

She is energetic and strong, a hard worker. (Proverbs 31:17)

My sheep recognize My voice; I know them, and they follow Me. I give them eternal life, and they will never perish. No one will snatch them away from Me, for My Father has given them to Me, and He is more powerful than anyone else. No one can take them from Me. (John 10:27–29)

Mom's Hands

"Hold onto my hand," my mom said to me.
Her powerful hand gave me comfort at age three.
She kept me safe and secure within her reach.
"Don't ever play with matches," she would preach.

Mom's hands at other times made me tense.
Fresh cuts dripped blood from fixing barbed wire fence.
Those hands put up tons of corn and apples too.
I recall how hard she worked, all the hay bales she threw.

Mom's specialties were her pies, buns and stew.
She loved to cook for guests, many times out of the blue.
She worked in the fields all day long
And climbed silos with hands that were strong.

Mom drove eighty miles an hour to my basketball game one day.
How those hands clapped with praise as she watched me play.
We practiced shooting everyday as she retrieved my ball.
Those same hands paid that speeding ticket, hidden from all.

When I was in my thirties, I asked my mom one day,
"When I was wild in college, how often did you pray?"
Mom looked me straight in the eye and replied with a glare,
"You'll never know how often I knelt for you in prayer."

Mom's hands wrote pages of Biblical information
As she watched her favorite Christian station.
She turned the pages of her Bible she read seven times through.
What an example those hands were for me and for you.

I sit next to Mom and hold her hand, ever so weak.
I know how much it comforts her even though she cannot speak.
That weak grasp she had yesterday is not here anymore.
I hold her hand in mine once again, even tighter than before.

Mom's hands were more precious to me than gold.
I suddenly realize Mom's hands now have turned cold.
I trust Jesus now holds onto my mother's hand
As He leads her through that peaceful promised land.

My mom raised seven children on a three-thousand-acre farm. Along with the work in the fields, Mom always had livestock to tend to as well. She was respected as being one of the most knowledgeable hog farmers in the state of South Dakota. When the first signs of illness appeared, Mom knew exactly what medicine to give the hogs to cure them. Mom's hands of love prepared many meals for her family as well as for several hired men. Mom's pie crusts and homemade buns were absolutely the best! I am so thankful for all of Mom's prayers for me. Leading by example, Mom's hands taught me to pray, read my Bible, and serve others. I am looking forward to holding Mom's loving hands again and enjoying her presence when I get to heaven, just as I'm sure she is enjoying her own mother's presence right now. How wonderful to know that God led Mom with His nail-scarred hand to heaven and that no one will snatch me out of His hand either.

The Lord hears His people when they call to Him for help. He rescues them from all their troubles. The Lord is close to the brokenhearted; He rescues those who are crushed in spirit. (Psalm 34:17–18)

When you go through deep waters and great trouble, I will be with you. When you go through rivers of difficulty, you will not drown! (Isaiah 43:2)

Prayer of Brokenness

My Lord, I thank You for staying by my side
And breaking all my stubborn foolish pride.
Though it is painful, I know
It is part of Your plan.

Because when I let Your Spirit take control,
The hot and stinging tears start to roll,
And I can feel You changing my soul
To be more like Yours.

God's refining process to make me more like Him includes my being broken. Jesus was broken to the point of being crucified on a cross for my sins. No matter how much I suffer as God changes my heart to be more like His, I will never have suffered as much as He did.

My pastor gave an example that helped me to understand more fully God's great love for me. There was a man whose job was to control a drawbridge, so that a train could travel over a body of water. One day this man's son was playing on the tracks of that very same bridge. As the train approached at a high speed, there was only enough time for the man in charge to either save his son or save the hundreds of people on the train. After a few seconds of anguish, the man lowered the bridge and sacrificed his son so that many could live.

Jesus is the bridge that closes the gap between us and heaven. He died so that I might live. Daily I surrender my life, my will, my emotions, and my body to Jesus Christ. I have to be willing to go to that painful place for God to begin my healing process. I trust that God will go with me, as He promises to never leave me or forsake me. Pain is only a bad thing if it is not submitted and surrendered to God. Brokenness is a positive thing when God uses it to allow His power, love and peace to flow through me more. The process of brokenness is His will being accomplished in my life instead of my own. Thank you, God, for the pain that has come my way. I have experienced Your presence and power in my life in ways I never would have known.

I will bless the Lord Who guides me, even at night my heart instructs me. (Psalm 16:7)

Don't worry about anything; instead, pray about everything. Tell God what you need, and thank Him for all He has done. If you do this, you will experience God's peace, which is far more wonderful than the human mind can understand. His peace will guard your hearts and minds as you live in Christ Jesus. (Philippians 4:6–7)

That is why we live by believing and not by seeing. (2 Corinthians 5:7)

Father Help Me

Father, I know You're in control,
But restlessness consumes my soul.
Help me trust Your sovereign ways
and always give You praise.

I'm so sad my life took a different course.
Help me lean on You my all-powerful source.
Every day of my life is in Your control.
You're perfecting my fragile, hurting soul.

Teach me to sit quietly and still
Help me surrender to Your will.
Guide me through my restless night.
I walk by faith and not by sight.

When I'm anxious and full of fear,
I read my Bible and You draw near.

Jesus is the source of my peace.
His presence makes my fear cease.

Thank You for Your faithfulness to me.
Though once blind, now I see.
Those who sinned more love more too.
This is my life, through and through.

I wrote this poem three months after Mom and Dad died. After having a six-week reprieve from work for processing my losses, I found myself facing another four months off from work after I injured my leg. I struggled with God's timing to give me more time away from work, which I did not think I needed. Eventually, I came to the conclusion that God is in control, and I prayed for His leading during my absence from work. I thanked God that I did not need a cast or surgery. I also thanked God for helping me discover my gift of writing. Prior to this I had not written anything. Never again in my nursing career will I get a four month block to strictly devote to my writing. Once again, I ever so humbly admit I do not know what is best for me. Dear Father, please help me surrender to Your will, every second of every day, so You may accomplish all the plans You have for me.

Give all your worries and cares to God, for He cares about what happens to you. (1 Peter 5:7)

Are any among you suffering? They should keep on praying about it. And those who have reason to be thankful should continually sing praises to the Lord. (James 5:13)

Mom's Prayers

Mom had a formula to pray
In her own special, loving way.
Mom would always be the one to pray
At holidays and loved it in every way.

Mom would begin with adoration and love
To God Who forgave her and was seated above.
She'd thank Him for all the miracles He'd done.
She'd thank Him for sacrificing His only Son.

Mom would thank God for food as we'd dine
And for God's great power to turn water into wine.
She'd praise God for making the lame to walk,
The blind to see, and the dumb to talk.

Mom would pray for God to bestow
Healing to her dear children below.
She'd pray for elderly who were ill,
Whose loneliness only God could fill.

She asked God to bless everyone.
She thanked Him for the death of His Son
Jesus Who overcame the power of death and hell.
Praise God! My mom is alive and well.

God is answering my prayers you see;
For out of my pain He sets others free.
Now I pray in my mother's place.
Thank God for His amazing grace!

Peace in the country
And unity in the family
Are what Mom prayed to Thee.
"Now You hear the same prayers from me."

Hulda lives in Bridgewater, SD, and taught Sunday school with Mom for over twenty-five years for the adult women's class. When I informed Hulda that I was writing poems regarding Mom, she told me I needed to write one about the specific formula Mom used whenever she prayed. That evening I prayed for God to help me and wrote the above poem. Mom's sister, Viola, always loved to hear Mom pray as well. On Mom's death bed, I asked her what she prayed for when she prayed to God. Mom's response was for peace in the country and unity in the family. I told Mom we were already working on that.

I thank God for whatever circumstances He brings into my life, the good and the bad. As more difficult problems surface in my life, the more I praise God. It is through praise that I experience the presence of God in mighty ways. I offer my adoration and praise to Jesus Who died in my place.

And I am convinced that nothing can ever separate us from His love. Death can't, and life can't. The angels can't, and the demons can't. Our fears for today, our worries about tomorrow, and even the powers of hell can't keep God's love away. (Romans 8:38)

For God has not given me a spirit of fear and timidity, but of power, love, and self-discipline. (2 Timothy 1:7)

I know the Lord is always with me. I will not be shaken, for He is right beside me. (Acts 2:25)

So humble yourselves before God. Resist the devil, and he will flee from you. Draw close to God, and God will draw close to you. (James 4:7–8)

Such love has no fear because perfect love expels all fear. (1 John 4:18)

Stay Close

The Lord is close when my heart breaks.
My fears, my troubles, even death He overtakes.
Nothing can ever separate me from God's love.
He's with me whether I am far below or high above.

If I wait upon the Lord,
My strength shall be restored.
Like the eagles I shall soar
To heights I've never dreamed before!

He holds me close but never against my will
Until I am calm and completely still.
He is able to do more than I dare ask or hope.
Many times He carries me so I am able to cope.

I bow my head in prayer upon bended knee,
So I can sail through that wild, raging sea!
Jesus makes my crooked paths straight.
I trust God to show me as I patiently wait.

No matter what your trial is, I have one piece of advice.
Don't ever give up your faith in God. Use it as a vise.
The rest of your life is built upon the choices you now make.
Stay close to God and thankful, even when your heart may break.

After a six-week reprieve from work when both of my parents died only thirteen days apart, I decided I was ready to return back to work. Shortly after, I was working a night shift and while walking down a long dark corridor, I started thinking about all of my losses. Suddenly I became overwhelmed and fearful. Immediately I prayed to God that I needed to feel His presence right then and know that He was near. Right after that prayer, God's love and peace flooded my heart as my fear left. While fear is from Satan, peace is from God. I thanked God for His immediate faithful response to my prayer. I experienced first hand the power of the Lord's prayer which states, "Deliver me from evil." Whenever I discern fear in one of my patients, I hold his or her hand and suggest we pray the Lord's Prayer together. God is faithful to come when we call on Him and His peace settles over the entire room. I thank God for taking away my fear as His peace becomes more and more at home in my heart.

Our Father, Who art in heaven, hallowed be Thy name. Thy kingdom come. Thy will be done on earth as it is in heaven. Give us this day our daily bread, and forgive us our sins as we forgive those who have sinned against us. And lead us not into temptation, but deliver us from evil. For Thine is the kingdom, and the power, and the glory, forever and ever. Amen.

Ruth's daughter, Brenda, her husband, Al, and their two daughters, Mel and Jesse, with their Cocker Spaniels, Maggie and Abbie.

But now, O Israel, the Lord Who created you says: "Do not be afraid, for I have ransomed you. I have called you by name; you are Mine. (Isaiah 43:1)

I—yes, I alone—am the One Who blots out your sins for My own sake and will never think of them again. (Isaiah 43:25)

He led them from the darkness and deepest gloom; He snapped their chains. Let them praise the Lord for His great love and for all His wonderful deeds to them. He broke down their prison gates of bronze; He cut apart their bars of iron. (Psalm 107:14–16)

Christlike

Do not fear.
The Lord God is here.
God calls me by my name.
My Savior always is the same.

While passing through waters I won't drown.
The raging rivers will not hold me down.
When I walk through the flaming torch,
Not one hair on my head will it scorch.

God created me
For His own glory.
No one can oppose His sovereign ways.
He is tomorrow, today, and always.

God's made a dry path through the sea
To lead His people to victory.
He blots out my sin for His own name's sake.
To forget them is a promise God will not break.

Thank you for the hard times in my life.
They make me Christlike through all my strife.
You promise to be with me to the end of the age.
Praise God Who freed me from my lonely cage.

When trials and tribulations come, how wonderful to know that God walks with His Bonnie through each and every one of them. Friends and family will always let me down to some extent, but God never changes. He is always faithful to love me unconditionally day or night. All I have to do is think about Him and He comes to me. My faith is built upon His righteous, faithful, loving and merciful character. How thankful I am that God cares enough about me to walk with me through the hard times so I am able to literally lose myself and gain Him instead. Out of gratitude to God for His matchless grace towards me, I want to obey, serve and know Him better each day. My God is a jealous God who says I am His. How wonderful to know He values me that much! He is mine and I am His. Praise God for Who He was, is, and always will be!

Difficulties in life at times make me feel isolated and lonely, that no one understands how I feel, and that I am trapped in a dark cage with no way out. When I begin to pray and ask God to help me, everything changes. Through the blood of Jesus, the door to my cage swings wide open. The light and wind of the Holy Spirit carry me to freedom and solitude. In Jesus, I am free from condemnation and captivity. Lord, help me daily to walk in my freedom and to remember that the only person who keeps me in a cage is me.

Forgetting the past and looking forward to what lies ahead, I strain to reach the end of the race and receive the prize for which God, through Christ Jesus, is calling us up to heaven. (Philippians 3:13–14)

For I can do everything with the help of Christ Who gives me the strength I need. (Philippians 4:13)

For the troubles we see will soon be over, but the joys to come will last forever. (2 Corinthians 4:18)

Press On

When you're afraid, press on.
When you feel defeated, press on.
When you've missed your goal, press on.
When you've hurt your God, press on.

When you've lost a loved one, press on.
When you've lost your hope, press on.
When you're tired and weary, press on.
When you can't find your peace, press on.

When your heart is broken, press on.
When you're alone and lonely, press on.
When you've been betrayed, press on.
When you've stopped dreaming, press on.

When you're discouraged, press on.
When your health has failed you, press on.
When everything's changed, press on.
When you can't find your way, press on.

When you don't understand why, press on.
When you can't feel God by your side, press on.
When you want to run away and hide, press on.
Until eternity, press on.

The difference between people who are able to cope and the ones who aren't isn't necessarily any particular set of circumstances. I have observed patients over the years with exactly the same diagnosis. One patient flies through the surgery while another can't seem to even get one foot out of bed. Perseverance and having a positive attitude will get you everywhere. Keeping a positive attitude while finding something or someone to be thankful for helps keep life in balance. I have found it especially helpful to remind myself that this life is only a snap of the fingers in comparison to eternity. Paul declares it would be far better for him to go to eternity than to stay on this earth. Be encouraged! The joys to come will last forever where we will be in the very presence of our Creator and Savior! For now, we will press on no matter what. With Christ's strength to sustain us, press on!

Bill and Ruth help Al and Dorothy Mammenga celebrate 50 years of marriage.

He reached down from heaven and rescued me; He drew me out of deep waters. He led me to a place of safety; He rescued me because He delights in me. (Psalm 18:16,19)

Then Jesus said, "Come to Me, all of you who are weary and carry heavy burdens, and I will give you rest. Take My yoke upon you. Let Me teach you, because I am humble and gentle, and you will find rest for your souls. For My yoke fits perfectly, and the burden I give you is light." (Matthew 11:28–30)

Letting Go

With tears streaming down my cheeks,
Both parents gone in less than two weeks,
I said to my friend, "It is well with my soul
Even when everything's out of control."

The key to peace is in letting go
Of all my wants and all I know.
It's accepting each day as it comes my way.
It's in caring about others by what I do and say.

I change what I can as I go on my way.
I accept the rest as God's will for my day.
I trust Him to do what is best.
In His sovereignty I surrender and rest.

When life overwhelms me with all of its woes,
I stay close to God and my anxiety goes.
I rest in God's presence and pray
For His comfort with each new day.

Nothing else on earth will ever even start
To fill this empty crater that dwells within my heart.
God's my only hope to be made whole.
He heals my broken heart and restores my soul.

It doesn't matter what hand I'm dealt.
It doesn't matter what I've felt.
It doesn't matter when I didn't take a stand.
What matters is that Christ holds my hand.

Even though both of my parents died only thirteen days apart, I never lost my peace. My external reaction was that of many tears and extreme fatigue, while my internal feelings were those of hope and God's calming peace. I was thankful for the faith both of my parents exhibited and expressed to me prior to their deaths. One week after my mom died, I lost two of my dogs as well. My dogs were my family. The combination of losses was unlike anything I've ever experienced in all of my life.

For eighteen hours straight, my tears streamed out after I lost my dogs. Only after I redirected my thoughts that my dogs were in heaven with my mom, did I experience any relief from my intense pain. When I start to cry with extreme intensity now, I pray for God's help and His peace settles over me. My body relaxes as He soothes my pain, just like He did now as I was remembering how much I loved those dogs. Without God in my life this pain would overtake me. I thank God for His evident power in my life as I entrust to Him my every emotion as well as every other aspect of my life. Thank you, God for loving me so faithfully and delighting in me.

I want you to know what will happen to the Christians who have died so you will not be full of sorrow like people who have no hope. For since we believe that Jesus died and was raised to life again, we also believe that when Jesus comes, God will bring back with Jesus all the Christians who have died. (1 Thessalonians 4:13–14)

Weeping may go on all night, but joy comes with the morning. (Psalm 30:5)

Now we live with a wonderful expectation because Jesus Christ rose again from the dead. For God has reserved a priceless inheritance for His children. It is kept in heaven for you, pure and undefiled, beyond the reach of change and decay. And God, in His mighty power, will protect you until you receive this salvation, because you are trusting in Him. (1 Peter 1:3–5)

Hope

I woke up early one day
Wondering did I ever put that milk away?
I opened the refrigerator where I found my mail.
On the counter sat my milk, warm and stale.

Did I even remember to eat today?
What day of the week is it anyway?
Did you call me yesterday? I'm not sure.
I can't even remember. Everything's a blur.

I feel so unsure of everything I do.
I get so scared and overwhelmed too.
There are so many decisions to make.
What will she wear? Who will sing at her wake?

My head starts to spin. I can't think straight.
Did I pay my house payment? I cry 'cuz it's late.
Nothing seems to matter right now.
I just go through the motions somehow.

I cry off and on throughout the night.
Morning comes. I can hardly face daylight.
How will I get through all those lonely days ahead?
It's all this emptiness that I dread!

She won't ever read my poems or be with me to sing.
There are days I want to tell her just one little thing.
She won't ever get to meet the men I will date,
Or the man I will marry if it's not too late.

How she loved that red wool coat!
Look at all the notes from her Bible she wrote.
There's a poem in her Bible where my hope comes from.
It tells me Mom's in heaven waiting for me to come.

When someone we love dies, life can feel overwhelming at times. Our bodies and minds don't function like we're used to. I have learned to lower my standards and not expect so much from myself when I go through the grieving process. I felt better after I laughed when a friend of mine told me she felt like I did every single day of her life! There's always someone worse off than you are, like that blind man on the street making his way with the help of his cane. I was at a concert one night where a little girl who will be living the rest of her life confined to her wheelchair sang,

"Give thanks for God is good." I spoke with her after the concert and told her that her singing brought tears to my eyes because it touched my heart. It's when we are weak that God is able to shine through us in mighty ways and make a difference in other people's lives.

This too shall pass. Adjustments will come one day at a time. Be patient and kind to yourself. Allow the good Lord to heal your pain. Never forget the great hope we have of seeing our loved ones again someday. They are not dead. They are in another place, and they would not want to come back. Thank you, God for this marvelous gift of our salvation and Your promise of protection when we place our trust in You.

I weep with grief; encourage me by Your Word. (Psalm 119:28)

Take delight in the Lord, and He will give you your heart's desire. (Psalm 37:4)

The Lord your God is a mighty Savior. He will rejoice over you with great gladness. With His love, He will calm all your fears. He will exult over you by singing a happy song. (Zephaniah 3:17)

Keep Trying

On the piano only one note could I play.
I had so much pain, but I tried each day.
Little by little I could play some more
As God my feelings did restore.

With the touch of each key
Came streams of tears for me.
My feelings were pushed down for so long.
I could only reach them through song.

I'd sing a little too as time went by.
Beautiful songs came the more I'd try.
After a while the process was through.
There was less of me and more of You.

You made my heart more sensitive and caring.
You supplied all the tools for my soul's repairing.
You've always drawn me to what I've needed to do
and helped me as I prayed every day to You.

I'm older now, and the tears still come.
At least now I know where they're coming from.
I thank God Who helped me through my pain.
To live feeling empty is a life lived in vain.

The key to life is to get up and try.
It will all work out as time goes by.
Just trust in God to cradle your heart.
His love and healing He will impart.

Music has always been a very therapeutic tool for getting in touch with my feelings. At the lowest point in my life, I could only play one note on the piano. After that, the tears started to roll. The next day, I would try again, and I would be able to add one more note to the first from the day before. This process went on until my pain was healed and I was playing and singing my Christian songs. Though working through my pain was a long, difficult process, the alternative was worse. To deny my pain, I also had to deny my joy, and I wasn't willing to sacrifice that for anything. All through college, my feelings would come to the surface, but they were two weeks behind whatever triggered them. What an incredibly difficult way to live! Now God has healed my feelings in every way possible. God has indeed done a mighty, miraculous work in my life!

Ron Mehl, in his book *Whispers in the Night*, describes *to delight* as being "to find strength in another as you step away from your own strength." One of Satan's favorite tools is discouragement. When we are discouraged, we often stop praying. Prayer keeps me connected to the ultimate source of power in my life. God, may I stay encouraged through my daily reading of Your Word. In the Bible, David knew he could always count on God's presence and strength. I have learned to put my worries aside and delight in God Who in turn delights in me.

Ruth and Bonnie enjoying the Christmas party provided by Avera McKennan Hospital.

For there is no other God but Me—a just God and a Savior—no, not one! Let all the world look to Me for salvation! For I am God; there is no other. I have sworn by My own name, and I will never go back on My word: Every knee will bow to Me, and every tongue will confess allegiance to My name (Isaiah 45:21–23).

God is light and there is no darkness in Him at all. So we are lying if we go on living in spiritual darkness. We are not living in the truth (1 John 1:5,7).

God's Healing Light

I bring painful memories of things not right
Into Your faithful, healing light.
You come and heal all of my pains.
Your boundless love flows through my veins

I trust Your power and I command
All powers of darkness before You to stand.
At the name of Jesus every knee shall bow.
That Jesus is Lord will be their vow.

Your almighty power is endless to heal.
How you love to reveal Yourself, and not conceal
The perfect light which shines through my past.
In Your bright light my darkness won't last.

Lord, You are merciful and want me whole.
You have control of my life and my soul.
I give You my anger, doubt, and fear.
I can feel Your presence ever so near.

Thank you for touching my pain one more time.
I am the branch, You are the vine.
I can do nothing without You by my side.
In Your healing light help me always abide.

God has given me an abundance of healing from emotional pain throughout my lifetime. I praise God for His almighty power to do above and beyond what I even imagined He could do. Jesus wants me whole, so I am able to lead others to their healing as well. Without Christ I can do nothing. It is only through His supernatural power that I could heal that quickly and that perfectly. I walk in the light which is the truth of God's Word, the Bible. Dallas, my Friday night Bible study teacher, taught me that he believes when Christ returns, we won't just slowly kneel before God. He believes kneecaps will literally break because we will drop to our knees so hard and so fast in the presence of God's tremendous power and majesty! We will be unable to stand in the direct presence of God. That same power is available to me now as His Spirit lives through me. Lord, please continue Your healing work in my life today as I walk daily in the light of Your truth.

And I will give you a new heart with new and right desires, and I will put a new spirit in you. I will take out your stony heart of sin and give you a new, obedient heart. (Ezekiel 36:26)

"I have told you all this so that you may have peace in Me. Here on earth you will have many trials and sorrows. But take heart, because I have overcome the world" (John 16:33).

But this precious treasure—this light and power that now shine within us—is held in perishable containers, that is, in our weak bodies. So everyone can see that our glorious power is from God and is not our own. We are pressed on every side by troubles, but we are not crushed and broken. We are perplexed, but we don't give up and quit. We are hunted down, but God never abandons us. We get knocked down, but we get up again and keep going (2 Corinthians 4:7–9).

Surrender

God carries me close to His heart.
He gently leads and my path does chart.
There's nothing even close to compare
With the awesome power I find there.

God places each star where it is to be.
He calls each one by name as He does me.
He counts them and careful attention does pay
To be sure none are lost or wander away.

God never grows weary or tired.
His work is to be praised and admired.
He sends His power when I'm tired and worn out.
More of Him and less of me is what it's all about.

If I surrender and God's Word heed,
Then I lose my chains and become freed.
I am like a grasshopper who has sinned.
God blows on me and I am carried in the wind.

I lay myself at God's feet.
What sweet communion as we meet.
He carries me in all His might.
When I'm with God everything is right.

I quit my struggle. The battle is won
Through the blood of Jesus, God's only son.
No matter what happens from this day on,
I've a home in heaven. My old life is gone.

My God is jealous regarding my time.
If I stray from Him and head toward the slime,
God pursues me with all His might
Until I am back in His holy light.

One of my faults is taking things into my own hands and not relying on God for help. I am a very capable woman, which has made it hard for me to depend on anyone to help me. Repeated situations came into my life where I have needed to surrender to God. There was no other solution that worked. I know because I've tried them all and was utterly miserable. When I was at the end of my rope, I knelt at God's feet and turned my life over to Him. Through the cracks of my life, His healing light shone through until He was at the center instead of me. By living my life surrendered to God, I'm never disappointed because He's in charge of the outcome from the time I open my eyes in the morning until I close them at night. I thank God He sought me and found me. By trusting God, my future is only limited by Who He is, and God has no limits. Lord, help me to be faithful to You today. Thank You, God, for overcoming the world and preparing a home in heaven for me.

I waited patiently for the Lord to help me, and He turned to me and heard my cry. He lifted me out of the pit of despair, out of the mud and the mire. He set my feet on solid ground and steadied me as I walked along. He has given me a new song to sing, a hymn of praise to our God (Psalm 40:1–3).

Do not throw away this confident trust in the Lord, no matter what happens (Hebrews 10:35).

For I can do everything with the help of Christ Who gives me the strength I need (Philippians 4:13).

Tears

Different circumstances over the years
Taught me there are different kinds of tears.
There are tears of joy because I'm so glad.
There are tears of grief because I'm so sad.

There are tears from being bitter that are hot and stinging.
There are tears from anger at what life is bringing.
There are tears of loneliness when no one is in sight.
There are tears of darkness when there is hardly any light.

There are tears from uncertainty and fear
As my loved one is disabled or no longer near.
There are tears of frustration when nothing seems right.
There are tears of abandonment in the middle of the night.

Whatever the reason for the tear,
God is greater than any person or thing here.
God is unrestricted in His power above all the rest.
His greatness exceeds any trial or test.

Though I can't see God, in my heart I know
He will protect me as in His will I go.
These emotions will pass, and I'll know what to do
As I read God's word to help me through.

God is sufficient to meet all my needs.
I pray with faith and God waters my seeds.
God holds me firmly in His sovereign clutch.
He gave up His only Son. He loved me that much!

You're waiting for that crucial test result. The results are negative and the tears flow. You're waiting for that crucial test result. The results are positive and the tears flow. Whatever the reason for the tears, how wonderful to know that God is always bigger and greater than any problem that may arise. I can do everything through Christ Who gives me the strength I need to get through it! But by the grace and almighty power of God I walk. No matter what happens, never give up your faith in God. It is at this point, the darkness may overtake your very life if you do.

God's loving, healing light protects us each day as we walk in it. Praise God who heard my cries for help and gave me a new song to sing. God has truly set my feet on the solid ground of His Holy Word. No matter what happened, I never gave up my confident trust that God would bring me through the raging storm one day at a time to quiet pastures once again. Thank you, God, that each day of my life is in Your hands.

Bonnie, her sister, Brenda, and her brother, Bruce, support-
ing each other through Christmas eve at Brenda's home.

When we were utterly helpless, Christ came at just the right time and died for us sinners (Romans 5:6).

He always prays earnestly for you, asking God to make you strong and perfect, fully confident of the whole will of God (Colossians 4:12).

God's Provisions

God has been so faithful each time
I humbled myself and let Him shine.
He sends the right person, just as He planned,
To help me and lead me with His hand.

There's always been prayer
From people God placed there.
God answered their request
To lean on Him and rest.

Joy comes during the day!
That mourning will not stay.
Pain never lasts forever,
If healing is your endeavor.

I asked God to fill me with joy.
My entire life He did deploy.
He's filled me with the fullness of Him.
What a change this life I'm living in.

I'm settled more each time
God's life entwines with mine.
Praise God who set this captive free.
Praise Jesus who died for me.

God has raised me from a life of depression to one of stability and hopefulness. Each time I was brokenhearted and on my knees asking for God's help, He always met me exactly where I was. The darkness left and God's joy and peace replaced my fear, doubt, guilt and shame. As I read God's word and obeyed what it said, God changed my heart and made it more like His own.

If you're depressed today and have lost hope, be encouraged! Nothing stays the same forever. Things will get better. Just be patient and trust that Jesus will meet you where you are and take you where He wants you to be on your spiritual journey. He Who gave everything He had, even His life, wants only the very best for you.

You keep track of all my sorrows. You have collected all my tears in Your bottle. You have recorded each one in Your book (Psalm 56:8).

For He orders His angels to protect you wherever you go. They will hold you with their hands (Psalm 91:11–12).

The Spirit of the sovereign Lord is upon me, because the Lord has appointed me to bring good news to the poor. He has sent me to announce that captives will be released and prisoners will be freed (Isaiah 61:1).

Tears in a Bottle

I have, over the years,
Shed so many tears.
So many losses break my heart.
I don't know where to start.

I feel so feeble and weak
As relief for my heavy heart I seek.
God, free me from this strife
That threatens to take my life.

God has kept all my tears.
He's felt them all over the years.
He has a plan far greater than I.
I'll understand more as time goes by.

There was a time I was drawn to say
Affirming things to a mom that day.
Could I have been her angel unaware?
I promised to uphold her in prayer.

God loves to reveal Himself to me
If I get out of myself enough to see
His hand in the comfort as a friend so dear
Holds me in his arms or lends an ear.

I thank God for those tears, every one.
It's only through tears that my freedom's begun.
God replaces my pain with His comfort and love.
He rushes to help me from heaven above.

If I draw close to God, He'll draw close to me.
Peace settles over my soul as fear and doubts flee.
Though I don't know how many more tears are in store,
I do know, on the cross, Jesus suffered more.

One day, in the mall, I was drawn to a young girl who had a little baby she was caring for. To slow down from my busy schedule and admire a baby was unusual for me. The young mom shared how her boyfriend had abandoned her and her daughter shortly after she was born. I told her she must be doing a pretty good job because her baby looked quite content and happy. My praise was directed towards her for even choosing to have her baby. She and her baby had just moved in with her mom. I told her I was thankful God provided her loving mother to support her as well as her baby. My prayer support was promised to that family before our conversation ended. God cared about all the tears that young mom shed and kept each one in a bottle.

I serve a God of compassion Who rushes to my side when I am hurting. All I have to do is call on the name of Jesus and He is present. When I am broken, the gates of heaven open. God's mighty power comes rushing to support, heal and direct every single aspect of my life.

For our present troubles are quite small and won't last very long. Yet they produce for us an immeasurably great glory that will last forever! So we don't look at the troubles we can see right now; rather, we look forward to what we have not yet seen. For the troubles we see will soon be over, but the joys to come will last forever. (2 Corinthians 4:17–18)

"For I know the plans I have for you. They are plans for good and not for disaster, to give you a future and a hope" (Jeremiah 29:11).

Live a life filled with love for others, following the example of Christ, Who loved you and gave Himself as a sacrifice to take away your sins. And God was pleased because that sacrifice was like sweet perfume to Him (Ephesians 5:2).

Fragrance of Christ

God is so near to my heart that breaks.
He's as near as the time it takes
To pray for God's angels to rescue me.
From my troubles He sets me free.

God sets me free from all my fear
As I exalt His name and It revere.
I praise the Lord all of the time
As out of my darkness I now climb.

God set my feet on solid ground.
What a faithful, loving friend I've found.

He pulled me out of that miry clay.
He led me with His hand all the way.

What joy and peace—this new life I'm in.
I hide His Word in my heart so I don't sin.
To give a future and a hope, you see,
Are the plans my Father has for me.

May the things that break God's heart change me.
To be more like Him is my plea.
May He grant me the fragrance of His sensitivity.
May God be glorified as others are set free.

When I placed God at the center of my life, everything changed. God's love and peace flowed through me and I started to see the world more through His eyes rather than my own. God's compassion and mercy are new everyday and have no limits. The price for following Christ is to experience my own suffering as He changes me to be more like Him. The more pain I experience in my life, the more my heart reaches out to help others who struggle. No matter how great or how many losses I have, nothing can ever take away the great hope of my salvation. Not only will those difficult trials come to an end, but they will seem so very small once I experience the fragrance of Christ's love for me in heaven.

And the church is His body; it is filled by Christ, Who fills everything everywhere with His presence. (Ephesians 1:23)

I pray that from His glorious, unlimited resources, He will give you mighty inner strength through His Holy Spirit. And may you have the power to understand how wide, how long, how high, and how deep His love really is. May you experience the love of Christ, though it is so great you will never fully understand it. By His mighty power at work within us, He is able to accomplish infinitely more than we would ever dare to ask or hope. (Ephesians 3:16–20)

"My thoughts are completely different from yours," says the Lord. "And My ways are far beyond anything you could imagine." (Isaiah 55:8)

The Fullness of God

My backyard is a hill full of trees.
Their leaves rustle in the midst of the breeze.
At the top of those trees way up high
A beautiful vine catches my eye.

It grows up to meet the sun's vibrant rays.
Then it grows down to my fence where it stays.
What beauty it gives as it turns in the fall
So many different colors. I just love them all.

Up the hill I searched until I found
A huge vine growing into the ground.
I decided that thick flourishing vine
Had been growing a very long time.

This is how it is with Jesus, God's Son.
The more I walk in Him, the more we are one.
I grow in the depth of His power and love
Until I overflow and tower from above.

My friend prays Ephesians 3 for me each day.
That vine helps me remember also to pray.
I pray for my loved ones as well
That deeper in their hearts His love may dwell.

I give God my mind, emotions and will,
So He can with wisdom and enlightenment fill.
I pray to know the hope God's called me to.
Freedom, suffering and peace He leads me through.

God is sovereign throughout eternity.
I have a home in heaven prepared for me.
All I have to do is ask and then receive each day
This fullness of God, Who fills everything in every way.

When I lost my loved one, nothing seemed to be enough to fill that huge crater of emptiness within my heart. I have tried filling losses in my life with the wrong things that were not in compliance with God's teachings, and my crater became only deeper. When I turned to God, whose power and love are endless, my crater started to become more shallow. There are no limits when it comes to God. There is no sin I can commit that His all encompassing love will not cover. There is no pain too deep that God can't empathize and heal. He can always do more than I could ever dare to ask or hope. These difficult times allow God's strength to flow through my weak body. It is only then that I get out of His way enough for Him to carry out His will for my life. God's ways and plans are always for my ultimate good and far beyond what I can imagine. It is not my job to question God. I need only to rest and trust in His almighty, unconditional love and concern for me today.

Brenda and her mom, Ruth, encourage Mel at a state AA basketball tournament.

But when the Holy Spirit controls our lives, He will produce this kind of fruit in us: love, joy, peace, patience, kindness, goodness, faithfulness, gentleness and self-control (Gal. 5:22–23).

To all who mourn in Israel, He will give beauty for ashes, joy instead of mourning, praise instead of despair (Isaiah 61:3).

Balance

If it's already good how can you make it better?
Satan knows your weaknesses to the very letter.
If he can't stop something good, he'll try to stampede it.
Keep your life in balance to stand against his hit.

Are you hungry, angry, lonely or tired?
How did you get here? Are you totally wired?
Continue to track how you act and feel.
Take a nap; call a friend; go eat that meal.

Whatever you do, don't run from your pain.
Forge right through the center and you will gain
Beauty for ashes like never before.
Around that corner what joy is in store!

Hold on no matter what.
He'll open a door if another is shut.
People tend to give up just before
God provides another door.

If impatience and rudeness to others I see,
It's a red flag that Satan's right behind me.
I open my Bible and read of God's love.
His peace settles over me like that of a dove.

Jesus knows your needs even before you.
Talk to Him often. He'll show you what to do.
If your life is off-center, redirect until you find
God's love, gentleness, patience and peace of mind.

The favor of God's Spirit overflows as you live.
His faithfulness and joy you freely give.
Self-control and meekness as well
Permeate your life as in God you dwell.

The Holy Spirit is a guide for balance in my life. When I am experiencing restlessness, impatience, rudeness or a lack of self-control, I immediately recognize I need to make adjustments in my life. I must decrease and He must increase. Generally I need to surrender a certain thing or area of my life back to God. I know I am back on track when God's wonderful peace returns to me.

In those days when you pray, I will listen. If you look for Me in earnest, you will find Me when you seek Me (Jeremiah 29:12–13).

The Lord is close to all who call on Him, yes, to all who call on Him sincerely. He fulfills the desires of those who fear Him; He hears their cries for help and rescues them (Psalm 45:18–19).

The Power of Prayer

"I should write a poem," raced through my head.
It would not go away as I lay in my bed.
Finally I grabbed some paper and a pen.
I wrote down the thoughts that came to me then.

I cried so hard I could hardly write
As God led me in His loving light.
He helped me release many tears of pain.
He knew the peace and joy I would gain.

God is amazingly faithful to me.
His hand in my healing so often I see.
His leading was evident each day as I went.
So many friends and so much support He sent.

There were many churches praying for me
As well as for my siblings and entire family.
I felt the support of their prayers holding me.
Strength came that could only come from Thee.

I still feel a strength that can come only from prayer
As my family and friends so lovingly care.
The mighty power of prayer is like no other.
It brings me through the loss of my dear mother.

Tears and pain used to be things that I tried to avoid in my life if at all possible. Now I thank God for the tears that roll down my cheeks because each one represents the beginning of healing. How reassuring to know that everything that comes my way in this life is first filtered through God's hands. Since God has allowed this difficult time in my life, He will also provide the prayer support and strength to get me through it. Some days I just go through the motions. I trust things will level out with time as I lean on the Lord for my strength.

My sister and I were sitting next to Mom's bed as death drew near. She had been in the hospital for fourteen days now and it had been only thirteen days since Dad died. We both gave God the glory that the only way we could possibly feel that strong was through the many prayers of God's faithful people! God held us in His almighty arms of love as He carried us through those long, uncertain, difficult days filled with pain. Many churches, family members and friends upheld my family and me in prayer. Thank God for each and every one of them!

Standing: Emma, Ruth, Teri, and Viola.
Sitting: Anna, delighted with her 89 roses in honor of her
89th birthday.

He sends His orders to the world—how swiftly His Word flies! (Psalm 147:15)

Her children stand and bless her. There are many virtuous and capable women in the world, but you surpass them all. Charm is deceptive, and beauty does not last, but a woman who fears the Lord will be greatly praised. Reward her for all she has done. Let her deeds publicly declare her praises (Proverbs 31:28–31).

God Himself will be with them. He will remove all of their sorrows, and there will be no more death or sorrow or crying or pain (Revelation 21:3–4).

To Be Just Like My Mom

I planted some roses for you, Mom,
Just the other day.
I remember last year when I planted your roses.
"They're just beautiful," I heard you say.

"Happy Mother's Day, Mom."
I cried as I dug in the soil.
I was sure you could see them in heaven
And share my great love as I toil.

How I wish I could give you a hug, Mom,
And gently hold your hand
As I'd parade you through our garden
And share with you the beautiful land.

"Thanks a million!"
I know that's what you would say
If you were only here with me
On this sad, lonely Mother's Day.

For just last month
God took you to heaven so you could rest.
You now have perfect joy and peace.
For me it was another trial, a test.

You were a really good mom.
You did your very best!
You took me to church every Sunday.
For that I know you'll be blessed.

As I go to church alone today, Mom,
Know that I go with you in my heart.
And from God's teachings
I promise I'll never depart!

For it's only through death, Mom
That you could see God's face.
It won't be long I'll be with you
In that beautiful, heavenly place.

My soul longs to be in heaven with you
Where the flowers bloom day and night.
There'll be no more tears,
And God Himself will be our light!

"You can never talk too much of the things of God,"
My mom always loved to say.
So I'll focus on the Kingdom.
To be just like my mom is what I pray.

It was Mother's Day morning five weeks after Mom had died. I was thinking about going to church without Mom and how hard it was going to be this year. On past Mother's Days, I had always bought Mom a dozen red roses with white baby's breath, her favorite. This year, instead, the day before Mother's Day, I decided to honor Mom by planting additional roses in our rose garden. As I lay in bed crying, I started to pray for God to take my pain away. The thought that I should write a poem started running through my mind right after I began praying and would not go away. I grabbed a pen and started to write all the words that came to me. They came so quickly, I could hardly write fast enough to keep up with my thoughts. I was crying so hard I could barely write. God gave me that poem to help heal my pain. I read that poem for several weeks after I wrote it, and each time I read it, I cried.

Brenda and I felt sad that Mom didn't live long enough to see the tulips bloom just one more time. Wanda, my co-worker and friend, told me the tulips never stop blooming in heaven. I look forward to being with Mom in heaven where neither one of us will ever shed another tear again. Every time God leads me to do something to further His kingdom, I talk to Mom and tell her she really would have liked that.

And their prayer offered in faith will heal the sick, and the Lord will make them well. And anyone who has committed sins will be forgiven. Confess your sins to each other and pray for each other so that you may be healed. The earnest prayer of a righteous person has great power and wonderful results (James 5:15–16).

But if you do sin, there is someone to plead for you before the Father. He is Jesus Christ, the One who pleases God completely. He is the sacrifice for our sins. He takes away not only our sins, but the sins of all the world (1 John 2:1–2).

Someone's Praying

Someone's praying for me—I can feel it in my heart
As all of a sudden Your love You impart.
It's like the flowing of a peaceful, gentle stream.
It gives me courage to hope and to dream.

Someone's praying for me this very hour.
I can feel Your strength and Your mighty power.
Thank you, God for giving to me
The many prayers that draw me to Thee.

Your provisions are without end
As time and time again You send
Just what I need before I'm aware.
You know because You've already been there.

Thank you, Jesus for knowing my pain.
You're the sinless Lamb without any stain.
You're thinking about me now as I write.
You watch over me with Your infinite sight.

Thank you, Jesus Who prays to God above.
I'm surrounded by Your mercy and embraced by Your love.
Bless and keep those whose prayers I now feel.
May they feel Your love and know it is real!

As I was sitting in my living room one day, I felt God's presence in such a mighty way that I just knew someone was praying for me. How wonderful to serve a God Who knows our every need even before we ask for His help. Many times in my life, I have limited God's power by not recognizing fully all He is capable of doing. It is even more remarkable that God, Who was perfect in every way and never sinned, gave up His only Son to die for me. God, please help me to show that same mercy to others. Once again, it is all about Jesus Christ and His power. Through the blood Jesus shed on the cross for my sins, God always hears my prayers when I pray. My ability to come boldly to God's throne in prayer has nothing to do with whether I have sinned less today or more than yesterday. It has to do with God totally loving and accepting me as He sees me through the precious blood of His Son, Jesus. Thank you, God for such a selfless gift of love!

But as people sinned more and more, God's wonderful kindness became more abundant. (Romans 5:20)

We are made right in God's sight when we trust in Jesus Christ to take away our sins. And we all can be saved in this same way, no matter who we are or what we have done. (Romans 3:22)

In His goodness He chose to make us His own children by giving us His true word. And we, out of all creation, became His choice possession. (James 1:18)

If a shepherd has one hundred sheep, and one wanders away and is lost, what will he do? Won't he leave the ninety-nine others and go out into the hills to search for the lost one? And if he finds it, he will surely rejoice over it more than over the ninety-nine that didn't wander away! In the same way, it is not my heavenly Father's will that even one of these little ones should perish. (Matthew 18:12–14)

Stands God

Between hope and doubt stands God.
Between light and dark stands God.
Between peace and fear stands God.
Between freedom and bondage stands God.

Between love and hate stands God.
Between acceptance and rejection stands God.
Between grace and judgment stands God.
Between faith and works stands God.

Between holiness and lust stands God.
Between spirit and flesh stands God.
Between humbleness and pride stands God.
Between surrender and rebellion stands God.

Between vision and blindness stands God.
Between truth and lies stands God.
Between worship and ungratefulness stands God.
Between life and death stands God.

God is everything good in my life. He has given me freedom from the many wrong roads I've traveled. How thankful I am that I serve a God who pursued me until he captured my heart. I used to think I was never good enough to be able to approach God and that I had to be perfect before God would accept me. Now I know the truth from the Bible, which set me free! Through Jesus Christ I am totally accepted by God regardless of my past. How marvelous that no matter how much I sin, God's grace always abounds more! How amazing that God rejoiced more over getting me back in His flock than He did over all the rest who never wandered away. When I surrendered my life to God, I gained a Father full of compassion and mercy. I am His most prized possession in all of the earth! How amazing that my Creator chooses to reside in me until the day He will take me home to heaven to live with Him forever. Thank God for His truly amazing grace!

Mel and Jordan gave Bonnie tremendous amounts of love.

A single day in your courts is better than a thousand anywhere else. (Psalm 84:10)

We know how much God loves us, and we have put our trust in Him. God is love, and all who live in love live in God, and God lives in them. (1 John 4:16)

For who can prove that the human spirit goes upward and the spirit of animals goes downward into the earth? (Ecclesiastes 3:21)

In that day the wolf and the lamb will live together; the leopard and the goat will be at peace. The cattle will graze among bears. (Isaiah 11:6–7)

Unconditional Love

*I believe that heaven will be
All my dogs together to see.
Their love for me will never fail.
It's so intense it's off the scale.*

*They gave me a glimpse of the love
That comes from my Father up above.
They loved me both day and night.
I was so precious in their sight.*

*They eagerly waited at my door.
When I returned they loved me more.
Jesus eagerly waits for His time with me.
He loves me as I am, so I can just be.*

They taught me how to love myself.
To be in their presence was infinite wealth.
Through filtered eyes my dogs did see,
Like those of God Whose eyes see me.

He sees me cleansed by the blood of His Son.
I'm totally accepted because we are one.
When God brings people along side of me,
May filtered eyes be the ones they see.

One night I had a dream and woke up feeling totally joyful. All of the dogs that I have ever owned during my entire lifetime were together and leaping into my arms. Dogs have always been an important part of my life. After a long, hard day's work, I would come home and cherish being greeted with their love. Even when I make mistakes, my dogs still love me. How amazing that even as much as they love me, God loves me even more! It doesn't matter to Him either how many mistakes I've made along life's way. Thank you, God, that there is nothing I can do that can ever make me lose Your precious love towards me.

God loves it when I spend time with Him. A single day spent in the presence of God is infinite wealth! His love for me is so vast and mighty that it is not even measurable. God loved me with the greatest possible love when He sacrificed His Son on the cross. May God's unconditional love and acceptance flow through me to every person God places in my path. May their lives be impacted to give Him all the glory and further His Kingdom.

Viola and Ruth holding Ruth's twins, Norman and Bonnie.

For in Christ the fullness of God lives in a human body, and you are complete through your union with Christ. He is the Lord over every ruler and authority in the universe. (Colossians 2:9–10)

He will feed his flock like a shepherd. He will carry the lambs in His arms, holding them close to His heart. (Isaiah 40:11)

I created you and have cared for you since before you were born. I will be your God throughout your lifetime—until your hair is white with age. I made you, and I will care for you. I will carry you along and save you. (Isaiah 46:3–4)

Hold Me

"Daddy, I know this is where I'm supposed to be,
But all of this emptiness is killing me.
Will You please hold me for just a short time?
I need to feel You here, and know that You are mine."

"God, in place of my loss Your comfort impart.
It's like a grenade blew up in my heart.
I need you to fill it, Lord, with You alone.
I'm claiming all Your promises as You sit on Your throne."

I close my eyes and You're here again.
I ask You to hold me as close as You can.
I wrap my arms around myself as if they're Yours.
Somehow I sense Your love and in it pours.

You calm my heart and my teardrops stop
As all my defenses I willingly drop.
I have nothing to fear with You by my side.
In Your love I surrender and completely abide.

I have You hold me until I fall asleep.
I trust You'll heal my pain and in Your presence keep.
I know tomorrow You'll still be holding me tight.
What would I do without my faithful Father's light?

I've always been sad that I never had a dad who wanted to spend time with me and get to know me. I searched for that fatherly love in all the wrong places. Through Christian counseling, I was finally able to discover what I was searching for all of those years. I was confident I had a home in heaven with Jesus, but I didn't have a deep, intimate relationship with Him. As I made Him the very center of my life and turned to Him to meet all of my needs, our relationship grew. I experienced a peace like I had never felt before. God comforted me through the loss of my parents, dogs, and my health. Only Jesus could fill all of that loss, pain, and emptiness in my heart. He has always been faithful to help me when I have humbly sought His direction and healing. Before I go to bed each night, I ask God to hold me and wrap His loving arms around me. Thank You, God, for all that You have carried me through so far and for Your promise to continue to carry me for the rest of my life.

I recently added another miniature schnauzer puppy to my household. When I hold Sadie Mae tightly next to my heart, an immense amount of love wells up from deep within. As deeply as I feel this love within my heart for my puppy, it doesn't begin to compare with how much my heavenly Father loves me! I am truly blessed!

To order additional copies of

$\mathcal{M}$ AGNIFYING
YOUR DAYS

Have your credit card ready and call

Toll free: (877) 421-READ (7323)

or send $11.99* each plus $4.95 S&H** to

WinePress Publishing
PO Box 428
Enumclaw, WA 98022

or order online:
www.winepresspub.com

*WA residents, add 8.4% sales tax

**add $1.50 S&H for each additional book ordered

The author invites you to visit her web site:
booksbybonnie.net